Sports Superstars

JESSIE DIGGINS

BY GOLRIZ GOLKAR

BELLWETHER MEDIA • MINNEAPOLIS, MN

Torque brims with excitement perfect for thrill-seekers of all kinds. Discover daring survival skills, explore uncharted worlds, and marvel at mighty engines and extreme sports. In *Torque* books, anything can happen. Are you ready?

This edition first published in 2024 by Bellwether Media, Inc.

No part of this publication may be reproduced in whole or in part without written permission of the publisher. For information regarding permission, write to Bellwether Media, Inc., Attention: Permissions Department, 6012 Blue Circle Drive, Minnetonka, MN 55343.

Library of Congress Cataloging-in-Publication Data

LC record for Jessie Diggins available at: https://lccn.loc.gov/2023040016

Text copyright © 2024 by Bellwether Media, Inc. TORQUE and associated logos are trademarks and/or registered trademarks of Bellwether Media, Inc.

Editor: Rebecca Sabelko   Designer: Gabriel Hilger

Printed in the United States of America, North Mankato, MN.

TABLE OF CONTENTS

A SKIING SENSATION	4
WHO IS JESSIE DIGGINS?	6
A YOUNG TALENT	8
A SKI SUPERSTAR	12
DIGGINS'S FUTURE	20
GLOSSARY	22
TO LEARN MORE	23
INDEX	24

A SKIING SENSATION

It is the final day of the 2021 **Tour de Ski** cross-country skiing event. Jessie Diggins is ready for the final climb.

The race begins. Diggins glides past other skiers. She races up the snowy slopes. She crosses the finish line after 36 minutes. Diggins becomes the first American to win the Tour de Ski!

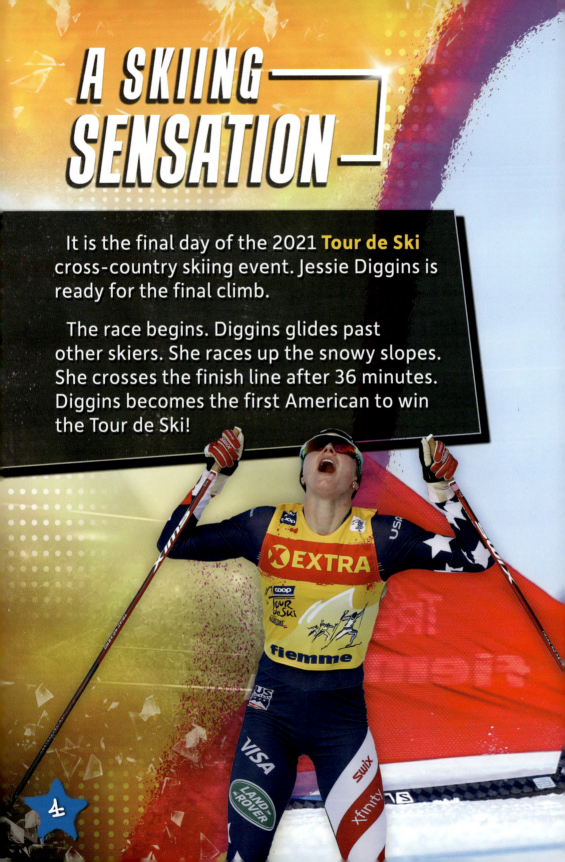

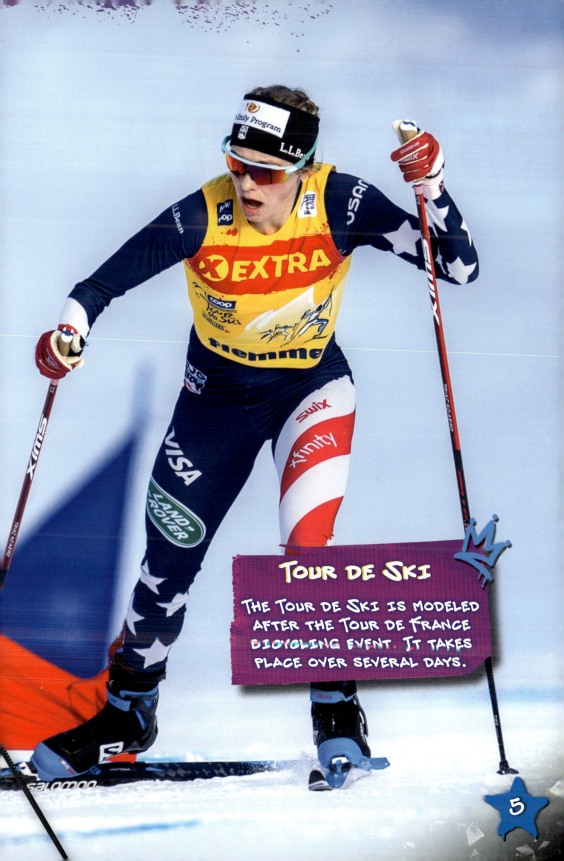

Tour de Ski

The Tour de Ski is modeled after the Tour de France bicycling event. It takes place over several days.

WHO IS JESSIE DIGGINS?

Jessie Diggins is a **professional** cross-country skier. She has won **Olympic** medals and world **championships**. She has won more medals than any other American skier!

Telling Her Story

Diggins wrote a book in 2020 called *Brave Enough*. It talks about her experience having an eating disorder. She hopes the book helps others.

JESSIE DIGGINS

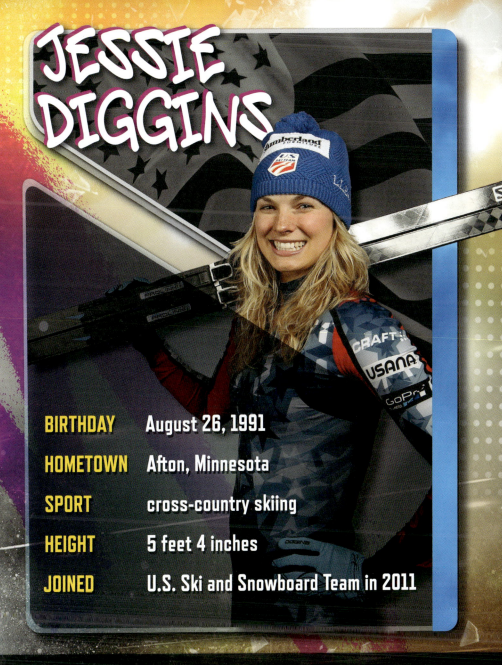

BIRTHDAY	August 26, 1991
HOMETOWN	Afton, Minnesota
SPORT	cross-country skiing
HEIGHT	5 feet 4 inches
JOINED	U.S. Ski and Snowboard Team in 2011

Diggins supports many causes. She works with a group that protects the planet. She supports groups that help children play sports. She also works to help people who struggle with **eating disorders**.

A YOUNG TALENT

Skiing has always been a part of Diggins's life. She began to ski at age 3. She practiced with the Minnesota Youth Ski **League**. She was skiing against older children by the time she was 11.

STILLWATER AREA HIGH SCHOOL

She joined the girls' high school cross-country ski team in seventh grade. She later became the top female high school cross-country skier in Minnesota. She won nine junior national championships by age 19!

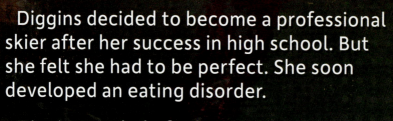

Diggins decided to become a professional skier after her success in high school. But she felt she had to be perfect. She soon developed an eating disorder.

Diggins got help for her eating disorder. She grew stronger. She raced with the Central Cross-Country **Elite** team for a year. She was chosen for the U.S. Ski & Snowboard Team in 2011.

FAVORITES

FOOD	HOBBY	PET	DRINK
dark chocolate	dancing	dog	coffee

Sparkling Star

Diggins puts glitter on her face before every race. It reminds her that she skis because she loves the sport.

11

A SKI SUPERSTAR

KIKKAN RANDALL

JESSIE DIGGINS

Diggins joined the Stratton Mountain School T2 Team in 2012. She began training with other top cross-country skiers on this team each summer.

She raced in the 2013 World Ski Championships. Diggins and her teammate Kikkan Randall won a gold medal for the **team sprint** event. Diggins skied at the 2014 Sochi Winter Olympics. But she did not win a medal.

2014 SOCHI WINTER OLYMPICS

Diggins brought a lot of energy to the 2015 World Ski Championships. She won a silver medal in the 10k **freestyle**. She won her first individual **World Cup** medal at the 2016 Tour de Ski.

Diggins won a silver medal at the 2017 World Ski Championships. She also won a bronze in the team sprint event.

JESSIE DIGGINS MAP

- World Ski Championships, Italy — 2013
- World Ski Championships, Sweden — 2015
- PyeongChang Winter Olympics, South Korea — 2018
- Beijing Winter Olympics, China — 2022
- World Ski Championships, Slovenia — 2023

2017 WORLD SKI CHAMPIONSHIPS

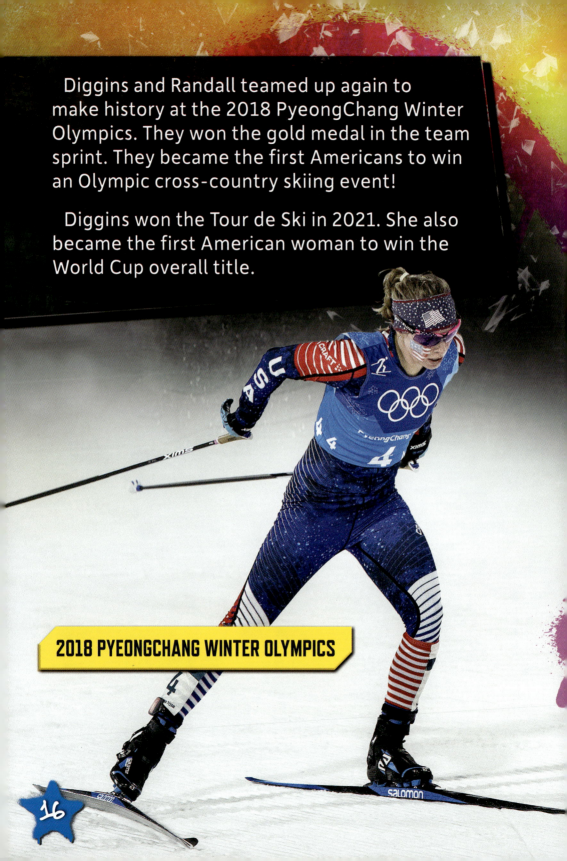

Diggins and Randall teamed up again to make history at the 2018 PyeongChang Winter Olympics. They won the gold medal in the team sprint. They became the first Americans to win an Olympic cross-country skiing event!

Diggins won the Tour de Ski in 2021. She also became the first American woman to win the World Cup overall title.

2018 PYEONGCHANG WINTER OLYMPICS

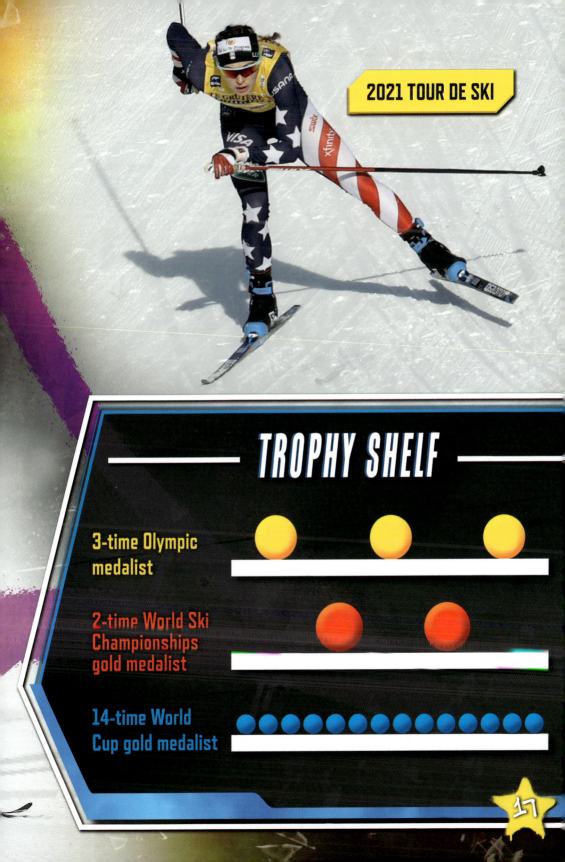

Diggins continued to ski well in 2022. She won bronze and silver medals at the Beijing Winter Olympics. She became the first American to win individual Olympic medals in her sport!

Diggins also won her fourteenth World Cup race. She broke the U.S. record for most medals in the **competition**!

2022 BEIJING WINTER OLYMPICS

TIMELINE

— 2012 —
Diggins joins the Stratton Mountain School T2 Team club

— 2013 —
Diggins wins her first skiing medal at the World Ski Championships

— 2017 —
Diggins wins two medals at the World Ski Championships

2022 WORLD CUP

— 2018 —
Diggins wins her first Olympic medal at the PyeongChang Winter Olympics

— 2022 —
Diggins wins two medals at the Beijing Winter Olympics

— 2023 —
Diggins becomes the first American to win an individual medal at the World Ski Championships

DIGGINS'S FUTURE

Diggins won a team sprint bronze medal at the 2023 World Ski Championships. She also became the first American to win an individual gold medal at the competition.

2023 WORLD SKI CHAMPIONSHIPS

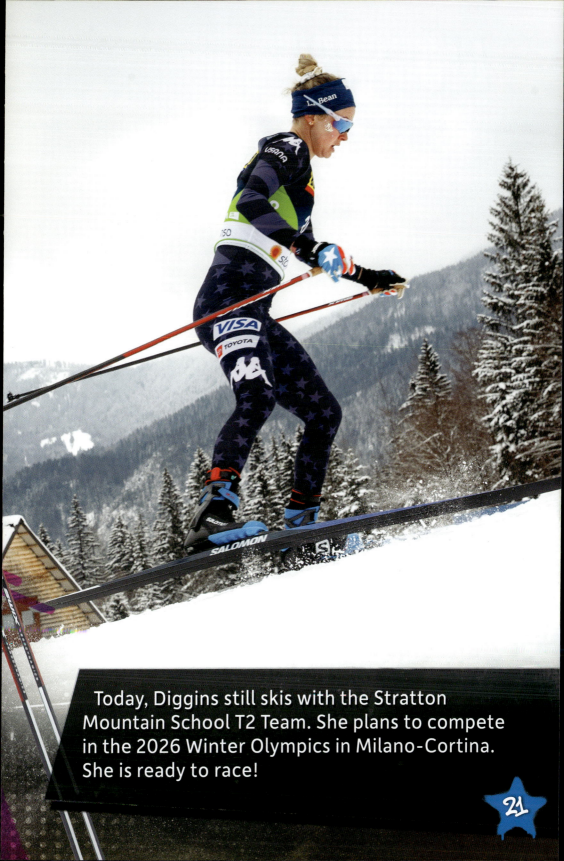

Today, Diggins still skis with the Stratton Mountain School T2 Team. She plans to compete in the 2026 Winter Olympics in Milano-Cortina. She is ready to race!

GLOSSARY

championships—contests to decide the best team or person

competition—an event in which someone tries to win something someone else is trying to win

eating disorders—serious mental and physical illnesses or conditions that involve damaging relationships with food, eating, exercise, and body image

elite—the best or most skilled

freestyle—a style of skiing in which skiers push off with alternate legs in a motion that is similar to skating

league—a large group of sports teams that often compete against one another

Olympic—related to the Olympic Games; the Olympic Games are worldwide summer or winter sports contests held in a different country every four years.

professional—related to a player, team, or coach who makes money from a sport

team sprint—a two-person sprint relay; in a relay, the first skier races a lap of the course and then tags their teammate who then races a lap.

Tour de Ski—a cross-country skiing event held every year in Europe where skiers compete for the championship during several days of competition

World Cup—a yearly cross-country skiing competition; skiers try to achieve the most points during a season to win the World Cup overall.

TO LEARN MORE

AT THE LIBRARY

Bode, Heather. *Go Skiing!* North Mankato, Minn.: Capstone Press, 2023.

Golkar, Golriz. *Chloe Kim.* Minneapolis, Minn.: Bellwether Media, 2024.

Sabelko, Rebecca. *Simone Biles.* Minneapolis, Minn.: Bellwether Media, 2023.

ON THE WEB

FACTSURFER

Factsurfer.com gives you a safe, fun way to find more information.

1. Go to www.factsurfer.com

2. Enter "Jessie Diggins" into the search box and click 🔍.

3. Select your book cover to see a list of related content.

INDEX

awards, 6, 13, 14, 16, 18, 20
Brave Enough, 6
causes, 7
Central Cross-Country Elite team, 10
championships, 6, 9, 13, 14, 15, 20
childhood, 8, 9
eating disorders, 6, 7, 10
favorites, 11
freestyle, 14
future, 21
glitter, 11
map, 15
Minnesota Youth Ski League, 8
Olympics, 6, 13, 16, 18, 21
profile, 7
Randall, Kikkan, 12, 13, 16
record, 18
Stratton Mountain School T2 Team, 12, 21
team sprint, 13, 14, 16, 20
timeline, 18–19
Tour de Ski, 4, 5, 14, 16, 17
trophy shelf, 17
U.S. Ski & Snowboard Team, 10
World Cup, 14, 16, 18, 19
World Ski Championships, 13, 14, 15, 20

The images in this book are reproduced through the courtesy of: dpa picture alliance/ Alamy, front cover; Tomi Hänninen/ AP Images/ AP Newsroom, pp. 3, 20, 21; Alessandro Trovati/ AP Images/ AP Newsroom, p. 4; Vianney Thibaut/ NordicFocus/ Contributer/ Getty Images, pp. 4-5; SALVATORE DI NOLFI/ AP Images/ AP Newsroom, p. 6; sharpener, p. 7 (American flag); Rick Bowmer/ AP Images/ AP Newsroom, p. 7 (Jessie Diggins); ZUMA Press Inc/ Alamy, p. 8; Chase Lau/ Wiki Commons, p. 9; Christof Koepsel/ Staff/ Getty Images, p. 10; irin-k, p. 11 (dark chocolate); Roman Samborskyi, p. 11 (dancing); cynoclub, p. 11 (dog); Visit Roemvanitch, p. 11 (coffee); Tribune Content Agency LLC/ Alamy, pp. 12, 13; Andrey Dmitriev/ Alamy, p. 14; CTK/ Alamy, p. 15 (Italy); Hendrik Schmidt/ AP Images/ AP Newsroom, p. 15 (Sweden); KoreaKHW, p. 15 (South Korea); Belga News Agency/ Alamy, p. 15 (China); kato08, p. 15 (Slovenia); GIUSEPPE CACACE/ Staff/ Getty Images, p. 15 (Jessie Diggins); Abaca Press/ Alamy, p. 16; Alessandro Trovati/ AP Images/ AP Newsroom, p. 17; Kirsty Wigglesworth/ AP Images/ AP Newsroom, p. 18; Kalle Parkkinen/ AP Images/ AP Newsroom, p. 19 (Jessie Diggins); Leonard Zhukovsky, p. 19 (Olympic medal); Rolf Simeon/ Alamy, p. 23.